FOREST BOOKS/UN

SO CHONG JU: THE EARLY LYRICS 1941–1960

So Chong Ju, also known by the pen-name Midang, was born in Sonun village in the North Cholla Province of Korea, in 1915. His first poems were published in the late 1930s, his first collection of poems dates from 1941. The present volume contains the complete poems of his first four collections, on which his reputation as Korea's leading living poet largely rests. In all he has published nine volumes of poetry, as well as many poems published separately. He has edited a number of anthologies and published works on literary history and criticism. He was for many years a professor at the Buddhist University, Dongguk University, in Seoul, where he is now Professor Emeritus. He has been awarded many of Korea's most prestigious literary awards. Translations of selected poems by So Chong Ju have previously been published in France, Spain, Germany and the United States.

Brother Anthony Teague was born in 1942 in Truro, Cornwall (UK), and has been a member of the Community of Taizé since 1969. He came to Korea in 1980 and lives in Seoul with other members of the Community. He is at present Chairman of the English Department of Sogang University, Seoul. Forest Books have published three volumes of his translations: *Wastelands of Fire* (1990) and *A Korean Century* (1991) by Ku Sang, *Faint Shadows of Love* (1991) by Kwang-kyu Kim. His translations of poems by Kwang-kyu Kim were awarded the Grand Prix for Translation in the 1991 Korean National Literary Awards. He was awarded the 1991 Korea Times Translation Prize for poetry for translations of poems by Ko Un.

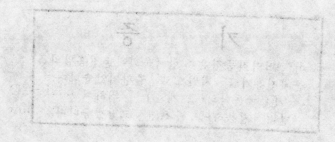

Midang
So Chong Ju

The Early Lyrics
1941 – 1960

Translated from the Korean

by

Brother Anthony of Taizé

FOREST
BOOKS
London & Boston

UNESCO
Publishing
Paris

UNESCO COLLECTION OF REPRESENTATIVE WORKS
Korean Series

This book has been accepted in the translation collection of the United
Nations Educational Scientific & Cultural Organisation (UNESCO)

PUBLISHED BY
FOREST BOOKS

20 Forest View, Chingford, London E4 7AY, UK
PO Box 312, Lincoln Centre, MA 01773, USA

FIRST PUBLISHED
1993

Typeset in Great Britain by Fleetlines Typesetters, Southend-on-Sea
Printed in Great Britain by BPCC Wheatons Ltd, Exeter

The publication of this work has been authorised by the
Korean National Commission for UNESCO.

A CIP catalogue record of this book is available from the British Library

ISBN 1 85610 025 1
ISBN UNESCO 92 3 102 889 8

Library of Congress Catalog Card Number 93-70421

Forest Books gratefully acknowledges the support of the Korean Culture and
Arts Foundation and the London Arts Board.

Contents

Contents

So Chung Ju

Introduction

In the late 1930s and the early 1940s, So Chong Ju (also known by the pen-name 'Midang'), startled the Korean reading public by his first, intensely sensuous poems. In those lyrics Korea found a new and quite unique poetic voice. The richness of a subtle vocabulary combined with sophisticated rhythmic patterns to produce works of remarkable poetic intensity. The poet was later to stress how great an influence Baudelaire and Nietzsche had on him in those early years; he experienced a time of intense inner turmoil, marked by hard drinking and sleeping in the streets. For a while he belonged to a gang of rag-pickers. He even left Korea and went wandering as far as Manchuria.

With the defeat of Japan in 1945, Korea regained the independence it had lost at the start of the century. Some of the poems Midang wrote at this time show more 'native' Korean elements, evoking a national ethos that the introduction of Japanese culture had done much to obliterate. Western influences combine with Buddhist and Shamanist traditions to shape the symbolism that Korean critics and readers have acclaimed in his mature work. Yet for many readers the first poems remain unsurpassed.

Still today, Korean critics continue to recognize in his best poems a quality that time and changes of fashion have not been able to reduce in any way. He is generally hailed as the greatest living Korean poet. It remains to be seen what his work can signify when it is read in translation; selections have already been published in English, French, German, and Spanish; now the complete lyrics of his first four published collections are being made available in this volume. The translations are as full and as conservative as is possible within the limits of the option to translate poems as poems.

Midang has made the ancient Korean kingdom of Silla a central symbol in part of his work. Originally founded in 57 B.C., Silla was a small kingdom in the south-eastern part of the Korean Peninsula, but by 677 it had expanded its control to cover nearly the whole Peninsula. It was marked by a rich Buddhist culture. Some of his poems refer directly to legends from that distant age, preserved in the ancient Buddhist chronicle known in Korean as Samguk Yusa (History of the Three Kingdoms) and other ancient texts. More universally, though, Silla represents an archetypal lost home, nostalgia for which raises the perceptive reader out of the limitations of the present into an awareness of eternal realities. So Chong Ju has written of his work as a quest for a 'poetic reconciliation of the present with the eternal.'

Behind many poems looms an intense sense of human solitude. There is one in which Midang recalls his first experience of that abyss of emptiness out of which his poetic energies have flowed, when he was only five. In several poems, he records a sense of standing before a closed gate, a door of iron or stone, beyond which the mysteries of eternity lie waiting. Elsewhere the barrier is a wall, or mountains, or sheer distance.

In his youth, Midang experienced the humiliation of Japan's attempt to destroy Korea's specific cultural and national identity. The radical writer and poet, Ko Un, has written a major study about the way in which So Chung Ju's early poems represent the Korean response of helpless anger and revolt in that situation. Yet by their poetic crafting, these poems transcend that particular historical moment. The role of the flesh as place of pain and pleasure, torment and rapture, takes us far beyond any simple nationalistic interpretation.

The overwhelming sensuality of youthful flesh is present in many poems as a romantic element that awakens the poet to intimations of the eternity contained within himself, a hidden vein of living, magic gold drawing his steps towards true being. Yet any experience of eternity must, it seems, be tinged with agony and death; this helps understand the dark, fierce tone of certain lyrics, the violence of many images. In the end, despite rapture, the longed-for light of the eternal land remains hidden, the doors stay closed and the senses too grow dull. The central core of flame is only perceived as longing and loss.

The climax of this theme comes in poems like that evoking the stone Goddess of Mercy, immobile and alone through the centuries, tormented by an undying yearning for intensity of encounter and life. Youth passes, and seems to leave us increasingly far from our goal. Yet in his poems, Midang represents a new hope, too. In the dark hours of midnight he seems to hear a mountain singing, his blood becomes a clear flowing stream, he finds himself flying with the cranes across the endless blue of autumn skies. In his most celebrated poem, the chrysanthemum seems only able to bloom because a nightingale has sung.

There is new serenity in the poems written in the 1950s, where small things, a cloud, a mirror, a flower or an embroidery, strike a poetic chord that reveals eternity as being very close. The cycles of birth and death surround him, the ice thaws on the river, and birds are born in the midst of snow. The blossoming of flowers, the play of children, and the inevitability of death draw together in a myth of natural harmony.

An important stage in Midang's development came with his discovery of native Korean traditions of simple beauty. For many centuries white was the normal colour of Korean clothing, and the main colour of Korean pottery. Such beauty he found lay close to natural beauty, and the natural sense of beauty inherited from the past became his guide in his journey back towards the mystery he knows as Silla.

The poet's quest for Silla is a search for a spirit that will transform and renew, not only Korea, but the entire world by its power. Very recently, in his seventy-seventh year, Midang set out to fulfil a long-cherished dream of living for a time near the Caucasus, in pursuit of the 'psychic residue of our ancestors' collective experiences' where heaven and earth and humanity once were one. This exaltedly visionary aspect of the poet's imagination has at times troubled even his admirers, many prefer the simpler lyricism of more modest topics.

In Midang's vision, all things are involved in an arduous journey towards an eternal land, while the poetic spirit writhes in its prison of flesh and time, longing for rebirth into a world of pure spirit. This may help explain his restless energy; each new period represents a new stage on an endless journey of discovery.

The poet's soul still longs to go sailing across the winter sky, free of the constraints of here and now, no longer young but ever young with the certainty of endless new things to be found. It is not by chance that the name Midang suggests an ongoing maturation, a process of ripening not yet complete.

Translator's Note

In publishing this volume, thanks must first go to the Korean Culture and Arts Foundation, the London Arts Board, and to UNESCO, whose generous assistance has made its publication possible.

The initial suggestion that I should work on So Chong Ju's poems came from Professor Taedong Lee, of Sogang University's English Department. He also enabled me to meet the poet and the three of us spent a most memorable evening together. In addition, the main ideas in the Introduction to this volume are drawn from an award-winning critical essay written by Professor Lee. I am deeply grateful for his help and encouragement.

Kim Kyung-Soo and Lee Dong-Chun, both graduates of Sogang University's Graduate School, rendered precious assistance along the way.

I am most grateful to Professor Young Moo Kim, of Seoul National University, for the long hours he spent going through my translations, correcting many errors.

Finally, I am deeply touched that Kim Jong-Gil (the pen-name of Professor Kim Chi-Gyu of Korea University), has taken so much time in his busy retirement to read my text. He has given me much essential advice, often helping to find ways of representing more precisely what was in the original poems. If these translations have any claim at all to be faithful renderings, it is in very large part thanks to him.

The inexact translations that remain, and the failure to find adequate equivalents for the beauties of the original works, must be attributed wholly to my own limitations.

Flower Snake Poems
1941

Self-portrait

Dad was a menial. He wasn't home even late at night.
Only old Gran was around, like a leek's roots
    and a flowering jujube tree.
For months Ma craved just to eat one green apricot. . .
And Ma's son, black-nailed under a tiny lamp in a mud
    wall.
Some folks say I look like her dad:
the same mop of hair, his big eyes.
In the Year of Reforms Grandad went to sea
    and never came back, the story goes.
What's raised me, then, these twenty-three years,
is the power of the wind, for eight parts in ten.
The world's course has yielded only shame;
some people have perceived a felon in my eyes,
others have perceived a fool in my mouth,
yet I'm certain there's nothing I need regret.

Even on mornings when day dawned in splendour,
the poetic dew anointing my brow
has always been mingled with drops of blood;
I've come through life in sunshine and shadows
like a sick dog panting, its tongue hanging out.

Flower snake

A back road pungent with musk and mint.
So beautiful, that snake. . .
What huge griefs brought it to birth?
Such a repulsive body!

You look like a flowered silk gaiter ribbon!
With your crimson mouth where that eloquent tongue
by which your grandsire beguiled poor Eve
        now silently flickers
look, a blue sky. . . Bite! Bite vengefully!

Run! Quick! That vile head!

Hurling stones, hurling, quickly there
headlong down the musky, grass-sweet road,
        pursuing it
not because Eve was our grandsire's wife
yet desperate, gasping
as if after a draft of kerosene. . . yes, kerosene. . .

If I could only wrap you round me,
        fixed on a needle's point;
far more gorgeous than any flowered silk. . .

Those lovely lips, blazing crimson,
as if you'd been sipping Cleopatra's blood. . .
        sink in now, snake!

Our young Sunnee's all of twenty, with pretty lips, too,
like those of a cat. . . sink in now, snake!

A leper

A leper mourned
the sun and sky.

The moon rose over the barley fields
as he ate a baby's flesh

and wept crimson like a flower all night.

Noontide

The path winds between fields of crimson flowers
which picked and eaten yield sleep-like death.

Calling me after, my love races on,
along the sinuous ridge-road, that sprawls
like a serpent opium-dazed.

Blood from my nostrils flows fragrant
filling my hands as I speed along

in this scorching noontide still as night
our two bodies blazing. . .

Barley-time summer

A stony stream burns beyond yellow clay walls,
heat bleaches barley that seems to hide guilt.
Where has mother slipped off,
leaving her sharp sickle back on its shelf?

Among the rocks where a wild boar once went
gasping, bleeding, along the path, the field path,
a leper wept, his clothes all crimson,

a girl stretched snake-like on the ground
sweating, sweating,
as I stood dizzy, she drew me down.

A kiss

Pretty girl, oh pretty pretty pretty girl!
Off you dash, out into the bean-field,
roughly smashing the fence down,
saying nothing except: Come come come!

Love, with love's pomegranate trees in flower,
west wind, stars, all laughing matters;
on each green hill a wild deer stands,
frog with frog, green frog with green frog

and the stream flows on towards the western sky. . .

On the ground, a long long kiss; oh, the shuddering,
biting wormwood, teeth so white set on edge,
bestial laughter tasting so sweet, tasting
as sweet as tears.

Pretty girl

Tears spring, tears spring,
as your hair hangs fresh washed,
you demand sour apples to bite; what to do?
This moonlit evening fenced in by the west wind,
gourd flowers white all over the roof,
nightingales calling under the leaves of trees far away,
insects buzzing, a flute sobbing,
a long hair-ribbon bright in the moonlight as deer call.
Your tears overflow though you gaze at the hills, the hills:
what to do, Yonsun? Your lips blush crimson.

Peach Blossom, Peach Blossom

I stand at a crossroads, cheeks burning
under a green tree's cool green shade,
gazing ahead, gazing ahead.

Jeremiah on my nakedness,
rapes on Piro Peak.

Out of the crazed sky
Ophelia's crazed songs echoing:

sweet foe, a moment of rest
in my pursuit of you.

A cloud shades my slight fever
so I'll flow on, still green, still green,
and setting with the sun, I'll come to visit you.

The legend of the tiled-roof house

The years lived by that lass, her eye-lashes so long,
a long ribbon, a long red ribbon in her hair.
The tiled-roof house's millenial arching Milky Way
has thickened blue, utterly blue.

That lass so shy, like shy fruit that trembles in any breeze.
The green snake.
The green snake that ate the mulberry fruit.
With a lantern hung from the indigo sky
pregnant with thunder,
with lightning and showers,

Sook died silently, coughing blood quietly:
she had lovely fingernails, they say.

A poem about my old neighbourhood

When I stand leaning against this icy stone wall,
I feel newly robed in fresh white muslin:
a weird sensation, as if I were back in old Koguryo,
native home of my soul, its eyes nearly closed,
and old words return like stars new emerging.

The evening lamp is already being lit. . .
I have wrongly lived for so many years!
Now I resolve to forget for ever the girls of Seoul,
sorrowful, tormented like Charles Baudelaire.

14, Sudae-dong, in Mount Sonwang's shadow:
a clay-built house, from my great-grandfather's time,
who used to make salt in the Changsu marshes;
my mother was expert at shellfish gathering,
and my father could hoist fifteen bushels on his back,

here ten years ago we two were together,
I and Kumnyo in her green blouse, March's Kumnyo
merrily laughing, a bridal pin firmly holding up her hair.

Soon spring will be back
and I'll get Kumnyo's younger sister,
her sister with the dark eye-brows.
Once I've got her, I'll live in Sudae-dong again.

Spring

Peach-flowers blossom, peach-flowers die, serpents wake, while over the west wind that brings emerald swallows, look, the sky, where ghosts dwell. The blood circulates well. . . if no sickness comes, my dear, then I must expect some sorrow, some sorrow.

River waters of sorrow

Somewhere, drizzle is falling
like tears shed by one kept from coming,
a twilight river flowing soundless. . .
only red red tears
soaked in dark crimson,
even when I try to smile,
by day, by night, at roadsides, too,
river waters of sorrow flow on,
ever surging on my brow. . .
in spring or on winter nights when lamps are being lit.

The wall

Weary of the wall I have been vacantly watching,
I kill lights and clocks

not yesterday, not tomorrow, not today,
not here, not there, not anywhere,

flickering like a firefly in the expiring darkness,
the grief of the static 'I'
the grief of the 'I' like a mute. . . .

When spring comes and azalea-cliffs flame red in the sun
I'll kick the wall and cry out in choking tones! like a mute,
Ah, wall!

A postcard sent to Dong Ri

With my hair crew-cut like this,
my face looks quite different from any other poet's.
I laugh with flinty teeth, the sky's so fine.
I'm glad to say my nails are thickening like tortoise-shell.

Until we're dead, old friend, and gone into our afterlife,
let's tell no more tales of nightingale girls.
Why did we pose as noblemen
like Li-Po with his long thin neck?

Even on moonlit nights worthy of Paul Verlaine
I simply plait straw with Bokdong the country lad.
If I hear faint weeping from distant China
I swear I'll cut off that shame-stricken ear.

A fragment

Nothing but the wind. Nothing but the night, and
    frost, and myself alone.
Let me walk, walk on, is my blood ripening in the
    pure blue sky as apples ripen? As apples ripen and
    drop?
Will tomorrow be that marvellous day? The day
    after that? Or the year after next?

An owl

I wonder by what perversity that cursed creature
visits us with its moping cry at deepest midnight?
It obviously bears some grudge against my father
and mother, against me and my wife-to-be as well.
First and foremost my poetry, then my features,
down to each single dishevelled hair. . . that wretch
has been spying by day as well,
like the shadow of far off distant darkness,
its cry a dubious spell. Though the blood-tinged surge
of the world beyond has soaked its wings, still,
its unclosing eyes turned heavenwards:
tu-whit. . . tu-whoo. . . Ah, owl, long ago
you built your round home in the darkness inside my head
    and came to live there.

From the noon-day hills

– to be like a gazelle or like a young stag
on the fragrant hills
(Song of Songs)

Do not behold with your tearful eyes. . .
this deep sweet trembling of boundless desire
or my lips' blood-moistened kiss tight
against the noon zenith with its raucous laughter. . .

Ah! How is it to be endured?
The sorrowful all went to Chinese lands,
but I drew honey into my heart
with whining wild bee swarms.

Look, lass, look how beautiful I am!

My complexion the dark tint of bark,
a golden sunblaze crowning my brow,

let's leap as we dance the dance of my stag
on this flowered mat fragrant with myrrh and musk

into the midst of laughing beasts, of beasts.

Ko Eul-na's daughter

There is suddenly laughter before me
so I lift up my drink-bleared eyes, and there
is a girl swamped in five-tinted coral;

has she risen from the sea?

How beautiful if I could glimpse in the sea
her hair, or her nostrils, her nostrils even.

Grains from the fruit of wild pomegranate flowers
on rocky cliffs, her lips. . . her teeth. . .

Tell me, by what name is that girl called?

Since there was shade, I seized her wrist:
I don't know. I don't know. I don't know. I don't know.

Eyes wide she goes racing towards the hills
and vanishes, singing barley-time songs when she's alone.

My rooster I

The flowery nature of a dozen equatorial sunflowers,
a night with the Milky Way heaving over kindled torches.
How did I come to love that sleeping rooster?

With nothing but our heads protruding from the sand,
at dawn we lie sobbing for joy,
our new-grown teeth all trembling.

My naked body, every nook and cranny,
is darkened to a persimmon hue. . .
The rooster laughs with a rustle of drooping feathers;

we're on good terms, like brothers sworn,
so with crests on our heads like national flags waving
let's crow out millenial Chigui Isle's noontide.

My rooster II

How is it that I long to drink the blood of one I love?
'Magdalene in a rock-crystal shrine!'

The rooster's comb is a flower blooming above its heart;
a cloud floats utterly drenched
yet seems Magdalene's bouquet of roses.

Wretched fowl, haughtily gazing around! Is the apple
of Creation's first age clean and clear in your eye?

Having already reached this peak,
how can love be compatible?

I'll slay you on a cross of sunflower stalks.
The murder of my mute silent fowl. . .

Dressed in Cain's crimson garb,
I feel how my fingers tremble and shake.

My scalp tingles at the taste of my fowl's fresh liver;
there, large as a cockscomb, a crest quietly emerges. . .

The sea

I listen intently but the sea and I are here alone;
though countless nights come and go above the ripples
rocking countless to and fro, always the path is everywhere
        and in the end is nowhere at all.

Your tear-drenched cheeks are veiled in night,
there's not so much as a firefly spark of lamplight.
Sink now, submerged with your flower-like heart
blazing alone in submarine depths of silence.

Play your four-holed flute, young man,
above the sea's abyss, the sea that surges
fresh and green, overwhelmed with passion,
bearing aloft the heaven's round.
Forget your father,
forget your mother,
forget your brothers, family, and friends,
last of all forget even your love,

and go to Alaska, no, to Arabia,
no, to America, no, go to Africa,
or rather, no, sink down down down!
With hair waving slow like blades of grass
        above the burdens of a dizzy heart,
how can my agony ever fill the sea?
Open your eyes. Open loving eyes. . . young man.
In mountain and sea, in every direction,
a fatherland lies, soaked in night and blood.

Go to Alaska!
Go to Arabia!
Go to America!
Go to Africa!

22

The gateway

To open your eyes alone by night is a fearful thing.
To open your eyes alone by night is a painful thing.
To open your eyes alone by night is a dangerous thing.

A beautiful thing, a beautiful thing. Become a flower
        lost in a vast ruined fortress!
Ah! This hour. Most precious of hours,
causing the hair to shake and move,
that must rise kindled above our dead flesh.

Bequeathing nothing but lungs and toenails
to a soul-tablet brimming with blood and light,
let's toss aside our clothes and shoes.
Let's say farewell to neighbours and home.

One unrepentant, unrepentant,
eyes wide open like those of a girl!

Come, burning, burning along frozen paths, a dagger
concealed in your breast; in the depths of knowledge
your cherished thorny gateway weeps.

Ode to the West Wind

In the wind gusting from the west:
fragrant spruce or juniper,
a dog-skin drum,
my woman's twirling ribbon twelve spans long,

deer, roe-deer, wanton deer,
the scar of your toenails,
the sound of a flute,

a blind man weeping,
the Goddess of Mercy asleep.

In the wind gusting from the west:
an ocean's madness,
a prison term. . . .

Resurrection

I have come looking for you, Suna. And I find so many of you here before me! As I walk along Chongno, you come smiling from all directions! Every morning, as the dawn cockrel crowed I longed to see you. It seems my calling reached your ears? Tell me, Suna, how many ten thousand hours has it been? After the flowery bier vanished over the hills that day, all that remained in my gaze was the empty sky: not one strand of hair, of hair to touch, only endless rain. . . . Once beyond the candlelight, once through the stony gate where the owls mope, the river flows for many thousand leagues; once gone, no news can return. On what rainbow then have you come down, descending from that difficult address? Here and there, glimmering at the Chongno crossroads, young girls approach, their voices chattering. Some of them are nineteen or twenty, too. . . Throned in their eyes, their veins, their hearts: Suna! Suna! Suna! You are all of you rising before me now!

Nightingale
1948

A whispered secret

Suni! Yongi! And Nam gone to rest!

Open your firmly closed ash-hued gates and come out,
see the flower-buds lingering at the fringes of the sky!

See the unfolding flower-buds cheek to cheek,
at the cozy fringes of the sky, tents woven
with endless silk strands for warp and weft.

Suni! Yongi! And Nam gone to rest!

See
the flower-buds breathing
at the fringes of the springtime sky, warm as a loving
        breast.

To a turtle

Turtle, slowly slowly paddling across the stream,
evenly quietly breathing, go ploughing on.
Go, parting with your claws the springtime petals
that drop to the furrowed waters like distant echoes
of secret whispers, then return.

Today my heart has caught fire again,
so that all my face is ablaze.
My speechless limbs are all a-tremble
like those of a new-born grasshopper
as the rays of the setting sun decline.

Turtle,
poke out and flourish your green head under the clouds
and I'll beat my drum,
I'll beat my booming drum, turtle.

Sunset has come for me and my brethren,
purple twilight glimmers on distant hills;
I beg you, though you may be hoarse,
speak one word with the old, age-old voice
of the blood that flows under your thick shell.

Untitled

Here may be rock's most solid heart, intolerably green. The green heart of rock that can never be ploughed by even the sharpest ploughshare blade.

Here may be the kingdom of heaven. It may be the grieving grieving countryside where grasshoppers sing in tender meadows.

Ah, here is how many thousand leagues away? How many thousands of leagues of hill and sea? How many leagues so dry I cannot cross?

Here may be a dream. A lovely lovely dream with even a tavern set beside a noble lady's tomb.

A flower

A flower has bloomed, sweetly sweetly bathed
in the gasping breath of people long dead.

Their dishevelled hair as it was in those days,
gestures and voices just as they were then:
here the songs of those long dead still remain.

Alas! Now their sound rings above the sky, the songs
those long dead used to sing, with their oily tresses,
each one sweating for heat, then gone for good.

Friend, let's rest before we go, let's rest, then go.
Here, in the shadow of this vast flower newly opened
let's rest, my friend, then go on our way.

Quenching our thirst at each spring we pass,
let's lean our chins on moss-covered stones
and gaze at the sky: one slip and we'll not see it again.

The Herdsman's song

For the good of our love
there must be parting, yes, parting.

There must be waves lapping up and down,
with winds that drive them to and fro.

For our love-longing's good
there must be the blue waters of the Milky Way.

In this lonely place of no return
there must be nothing but one body ablaze!

Dear Lady Weaver, alone here on the sparkling sands
I'll count the blades of grass that sprout,

while high above in the white white clouds
you pass your shuttle in the loom.

Until the seventh month's seventh day returns
and the half-moon hangs, a brow arching in the sky,

I'll pasture my black cow
and you, Lady Weaver, shall weave your silken cloth.

Revolution

The red and green pattern mottling the shell
is the sea's hope, the sea's,
that has seethed alone for thousands of years.

The flowers that unfold till the branches crack
are the wind's hope, the wind's,
that comes and whispers here day after day.

Ah! The revolution now spreading like a flood
across our land with its crimson servitude
is truly heaven's own long-kept hope.

A song of the Goddess of Mercy
in the Stone Cavern

Here I have long stood, yearning
with a yearning like that of the tide.

Deep in the cracks between stone and cold stone
under the tangled arrowroot vines
stirs a fresh breath of youth: that still is mine.

Until time reduces me to useless dust,
for ever returns me to the void, the void,
the waves contained in this swelling heart
and this love: they still are mine.

Days that dawn in the busy wind!
Marvellous Silla buried deep underground!
Flowerlike people buried deep underground!

Oh! If only He would come to birth, come to birth,
that One who loves me more than I,
that One who loves a thousand years, a thousand years,
if only He would come to birth anew in the sunlight,

if only, once born anew in the sunlight
he would drive me away, away into the dark.

I love you. . . I love you. . .
if only, having once spoken those words to my Love,
if only I could return to the sea!

So I have stood here by Buddha's seated statue,
with a tiny incense sack in my loin,

breathing in and out, as day follows day,
inside this cold rock,
with a fresh breath of youth, alas, still mine.

An alley

This alley that I frequent day after day.
This alley I step into alone early in the morning,
to which I return gently humming at sunset.

This alley where poor, lonely, waning people
come and go hunched, their eyes to the ground.

The ungrieving blue sky
covers this alley like a sheet,
on the rooftops white gourd flowers bloom;

as if this alley were soon to be swept away,
in every corner grief seeps like a rising tide;
if the wind blows, the shacks just shake in the breeze.

This alley where peddlars live, Palman and Bokdong.
Until I'm old, I'll love this alley,
I'll live in this alley until I die.

Nightingale

The path my love took is speckled with tears.
Playing his flute, he began the long journey
to western realms, where azalea rains fall.
Dressed all in white so neat, so neat,
my love's journey's too long, he'll never return.

I might have tressed shoes or sandals of straw
woven strand by strand with all our sad story.
Cutting off my poor hair with a silver blade,
I might have used that to weave sandals for him.

In the weary night sky, as silk lanterns glow,
a bird sings laments that it cannot contain,
refreshing its voice in the Milky Way's meanders;
eyes closed, intoxicated with its own blood.
My dear, gone to heaven's end alone!

Open the door

Your pale breast grows colder and colder,
though I bathe it with tears, to no avail:
will it gain warmth if I rub it with this flower?

I've prayed and prayed, for nine days and nights,
but your azure breath still flees away:
will it return if I rub it with this flower?

High up in the sky, in the Milky Way,
where pairs of wild geese plough the frost,
ah! that desolate flower-bed, blue and red!

Open the door! I beg you, open the door!
Dearest lord, my love!

Cotton flowers

Sister!
I feel tears rising.

Red and white cotton flowers soak meekly
in the azure above that pools like well-water;
sister,
you brought them to bloom, didn't you?

That autumn azure's so taut it would ring at a touch;
there even the rocks are falling, crumbling. . . .

Passing through drug-like spring,
on through senseless summer,
up and down the plantain-choked road,
bending your back, you brought them to bloom, didn't
          you?

Sister's house

Ninety thousand leagues across the sea,
ninety thousand leagues beyond the hills,
if there you climb down, a lamp in your hand,
    you'll find a well of water.

If you sink a thousand fathoms down
into the water's inky depths,
there you'll find, like an oyster shell,
    a robber's den concealed.

Open the main gate, open the middle gate,
open the gate of stone;
if you turn into wind and slip through the crack,
    there you'll find my sister so dear.

The robber's away,
my sister's alone,
sitting in white at her mirror there.

Azure day

On days of dazzling azure
I must yearn for the one I love.

In the place where autumn flowers bloomed,
green wearily fades into red or brown.

What shall we do when it snows?
What shall we do when spring comes again?

Suppose I die, and you survive!
Suppose you die, and I survive!

On days of dazzling azure
I must yearn for the one I love.

Stay at home

Little girl, little girl,
stay at home.

Stay at home
where the dandelions bloom.

Picking plantains,
plaiting sandals,

gazing at far away mountains
pale beyond yellow bamboo groves,

no matter how sad, how sad:
stay at home.

Returning to Soguipo

Like a cuckoo weeping then wiping its eyes
at the sight of leaves so thickly sprouting
deep in the hills,

like a west wind, a south wind,
a whirlwind,
like the fish that glide in the ocean flood,

today I'm going to Soguipo.
Limbs swinging, I'm off to Soguipo.

Clouds rise
with every step I take,

wings sprout
at my panting breath,

today I'm going to Soguipo,
to Soguipo, to see you.

A red sky

The river flows westwards,
the wind flows through willow trees,

on a meadow path with fresh flowers blooming
we stand brushing tears away, about to part,
and above our heads the clouds flow by,

your two red cheeks,
your panting breath,
your love, and vows all flow away,

in this autumn dusk with its falling leaves
I must watch the red glow of the sky alone.

A little song

What's that you say?
Ah, sky, blue sky,
too near,
you drive me mad!

I, always I,
never hungry for more,
standing on tiptoe,
am turned to stone.

A march

The feast is over. We sit for a final dish of broth,
letting the red fire burn down,
leaving only ash.

I push aside the awning: look, the darkening sky!
Let's stand up and take our leave.

At last, just a fraction drunk,
we all become people returning home:

Such is life!
Such is life!
Such is life!
Such is life!

I batter my bell, its clanging drops
on the sea water standing far away.

Dandelion

You fool! A white dandelion's bloomed.
Under a sky that makes you weep,
tee hee! You fool! hee hee! how droll!

People, like a team of acrobats, in pants
with blood-stained belts around their waists,
are panting away: if ever we're caught, oh dear!

Collapsing in a convenient barley field,
they loose eyes and noses, and love dreams too,

like liquor, like liquor,
I too will evaporate and drift blue in the air.

In Manchuria

My! This is too much sky. If I were to go rushing away, where would I go? It would be easy to go mad here, mad as red cloth. For how many thousands of years, thousands of years, have these people been living at leisure alone!

There is a drum here, rather than a bell. Is that a kind of inevitable extravagance, that cannot be heard from far away? There was no last name to be called, really. How is it that when you see me, when I see you, we cannot help laughing?

Strictly speaking, there was nothing like Harbin City at all. To you and to me, there was nothing like that. There was nothing at all, no scent of early peach-blossom, no sound of speaking, no disease.

At nightfall

At nightfall, dear Sook, I remember you. Tiny and neat
as a rocambole corm, I recall every inch of you:
the curve of your hair and eyes, your nose, your waist,
the length of your body, your hair, your neck,
yes, the length of your neck, uniquely slender,
and the sorrowful voice that rang out from it.

Those sorrowful notes, a cuckoo's call in an ancient tongue.
Day after day the sun rose and set inside the hard stone,
over the yellow clay fields and the standing well-waters,
the ticking of an ancient clock, the hands of that clock,
crumbling stones, mother's relics, your swollen red eyes,
leaving a red twilight glow, your inner parts
          drenched only in darkness, and your hunger.

The pine-tree branches in the grove behind,
with cords of yellow straw wound around them,
the murky slowly turning clouds, dark clouds,
with inside them a voice calling, calling my name,
repeatedly calling, like the name of a flower:
your decease, perhaps?

Perhaps,
perhaps,
perhaps,

ah, you too, daughter of those who flee!
Trailing rubber slippers with their black turtle mark,
trailing worn-out slippers over mountain roads,
steep mountain passes where rushes wave, then
you could go any way you chose.
In places all are brought together, travelling third-class,
going on foot, by steamer too,
in Mokpo or Kunsan. Anywhere

somewhere up the countless alleys there
in the monstrous buildings, mushrooming homes,
all those houses with lights clicking on and off,
the Stock Company Limited,
the Public and Private Monetary Fund,
the Evangelical Chapel, a bell ringing for Mass,
obscene whorehouses, the people there, people, people,

and finally, by your suicide. . . .

At the lowest levels of ferro-cement, ferro-cement,
where countless abacus beads, screws and cog-wheels
        hang,

maybe in some grim inner room of an employment agent's
you were forced to remove even your underclothes,
completely, those underclothes beneath your skirt.
You clutched and clutched with your ten dark nails
but at last, in the end, you were forced to go.

Ah, Sook!

Something calling me, in a thin voice like a live cricket's,
in the night of the wall of the night in this night.
Something calling me, with two rows of pure white teeth,
from Chungchong Province, from Cholla Province,
from some family-run wineshop in a rainswept port,
from the depths of my spinal cord, in fact.
Something calling me in the voice of sad humanity.
Endlessly calling like a bell or like an electric wire.

Like the sea, blue-black, or a splendid ovation,
like blood,
like blood,

flowing, moist, at the tip of my knife.

Sook! Now I'm through with remembering you;
I'm wiping my dagger's steel-blue blade.

Neap tide

Scrabbling through the tidal slime,
catching things like tiny crabs to eat,
shall we go mad at lean yellow neap tide?

The faithful sea waters that had sworn to meet us
came as far as our chins, but alas
the reins were not loosed, we could not go.

As we stand weeping like pillars of fire,
look, an extra toe-nail has sprouted.

Ah! We'll simply choke parched, and sweat,
and set like the sun on the neap tide's steep climb;
we'll never, ah never, meet again.

Travellers' rest

Pursued along side-ways and by-ways,
when I emerge after flailing through brambles,
my legs are torn to a raw red hash
and the stones grow wet with drops of blood. . .

when tears rise, since there is no one near
I go dashing onwards at random,
devouring all the tart wild berries my hands can reach.

As I eat wild scarlet-tinged berries in days of wild birdsong,
then gaze at the sun,
my sight grows clear.

Let's forget. Let's forget.
Father, mother, and wife, beneath pale paper lanterns,
their mournful customs, their sorrowful speech,
all tossed away like torn white clothes;
now my stomach must resemble some fierce leopard.

Though iron bars enclose me here and there for a time,
once out, my spikes grow more piercing than ever!
Though they dress me again in thin red clothing,
my hope is a blazing sea beyond red hot desert sands!

I'll go, I'll go on, entrusting to heaven each flower-like age,
every step passing beyond sand-dunes. . . sand-dunes. . .
where they say vipers' eyes lie buried bright like stars

for though I lie in some vast flower's shadow,
a skeleton simply scoured by the blue-tinted wind,
my heart's desire must ever be lasting joy.

Why do I so want to live?

> *– Hanging her basket on an empty branch,*
> *where, ah where has my true love gone?*
> *(O Il-do)*

When nothing at all is possible, I think of home.

I recall long-lost shapes that can never return, the forms of things that have vanished like mist.

Voices brush past, whispering faintly in my ears, voices echo ringing from some dark, far off world, but no single word is clear.

Yet still I can sense the sound of your breathing. Dear girls! where are you resting? I only feel my youth restored by the warmth of your breath.

What was it you once said to me, girls?

In the sky, that is now as it was in the beginning, a skylark draws a slender brush-stroke of blood, then flows away engulfed in clouds, while I strive to grasp the delight of a life I cannot live as I would, standing again before the still tightly closed stone gates of the journey ahead.

*

I was standing on a sloping road that ran between the barley fields covered by the afternoon shadows of the hills, following behind those four young girls: Sopsopy and Suny, Puchopy and Sunnye. That day, they were wearing bright-coloured blouses, crimson, azure, and white, like the four seas of legends.

From above came the distant sound of a horn. Sunnye said it was the horn of God. Each of the four girls bore a basket, bent her back, yet they were not really looking for plants but bowing. Not gathering herbs, dandelions and such, but listening to that far off horn. Each lowered her head with a look of regret.

Yet there was something that I could not grasp. No matter how softly I might tread, there was something that I could not grasp.

It only spread a clear long-lasting fragrance as I kicked at the clumps of dandelion flowers; it hid behind the dog-rose hedge and sped on its way much faster than I. The louder the voice of my calling became, the further it sped away.

Don't come here. . . Don't come here. . .

Laughing softly, it flowed away like a stream, like four little streams.

One scrap of memory: my two hands held high, for up there in the sky one single skylark. . . that alone remained, as everything flowed quietly away, murmuring. Don't come here. . . Don't come here. . .

*

Dear girls! the day when I must depart, will you come back again? Will you return, when I must go for ever? Will you pour out happy tears like Mary of Magdala, and wipe my fingertips with your hair?

*

Why, when I pricked myself on a thorn, in my pain the four of them used to come and stand beside me. When I cut myself on a rose thorn or a shard, in my pain they would come to make it better with mother-like fingers.

When my childhood blood pearled at fingers' ends, if one of them cared the others cared too, and strange to say, my scratches would always heal, whether they were rubbed with a yellow flower, with a white flower, or a red!

Lord Chong! my love! Lord Chong!
Your sweetheart has come, so open the door!

If you rub with a red flower
red blood returns,
with an azure flower
azure breath returns.

*

Dear girls! why is the sky so blue when the
rain-clouds have gone? Why can I hear so clearly a
sound of breathing? Why do I so want to live? Has my
breast been rubbed with some flower?

*

Standing in a meadow at the foot of a cliff where a
few sparse dandelions bloom, a mere soul, I invoke
those little girls.
I am sure they have been protecting me. If only
this rain falling inside me would stop, if I could only
go back and stand again on that sloping road, if only
this sickness could quickly be made well: all they
were always waiting for, always, on that long-ago
barley-field path.

*

The day when I must depart for ever, will you come
back again?

54

Selected Poems of So Chong Ju
1955

On seeing Mudung Mountain

Poverty's no more than ragged clothes.
Can it conceal our natural flesh and natural mind?
They're like the mountain in summer
standing with dark green ridges exposed in dazzling
    sunlight.

All we can do is raise our children
as the green hill raises herbs and orchids in its lap.
When afternoon comes,
bringing life swirling and rolling,
you husbands and wives
must sometimes sit,
sometimes rather lie side by side.

The wife should gaze into her husband's eyes,
the husband put a hand on his wife's brow.

Even laid in thorny wormwood ditches,
we should always think we're like buried jewels
and gather green moss thickly over us.

The crane

The crane flies on
like a smooth river flowing,
no ripples lapping,
through a thousand years of care.

Eyes that have seen a thousand years,
wings that have beaten a thousand years
strike once again against heaven's end

yet the fury that should be vast as mountains,
the sorrow that should make the very trees weep
just flow on so peacefully!

Look: pale jade and crimson red!
Look: pale jade and crimson red!
As we inspect our sister's embroidery,
let's inspect the world;

as we inspect her embroidered flowers,
gazing over her shoulder,
let's inspect the world.

Tears like a tidal wave
or a solemn service for the dead,

a dance, can't you dance any time you choose?
Instead of burying your head under your wing, silent,
a dance: can't you dance any drinking time you choose?

What could not be done by tears, by dancing, by enduring,
goes flying at the verge of the world beyond
caressingly, caressingly,
wrapped in clouds that slowly then more quickly rock.

Beside a chrysanthemum

For one chrysanthemum to bloom
the nightingale
must have sung like that since spring.

For one chrysanthemum to bloom
the thunder
must have rolled like that in pitch black clouds.

Chrysanthemum! You look like my sister
standing before her mirror, just back
from far away, far away byways of youth,
where she was racked with longing and lack.

For your yellow petals to bloom
the frost must have come down like that last night
and I was not even able to get to sleep.

Haze

A haze rises.
Looking like sorrowful dishevelled love,
delicately trembling, it rises.

The haze rising over Kongdok-dong
looks like the love of someone living in Kongdok-dong.
The haze rising over Malli-dong
looks like the love of someone living in Malli-dong.

Above the roof of the house where Suni lives
Suni's haze rises
and above the roof of the house where Bokdong lives
Bokdong's haze rises.

In the room where you embroider, sister,
a haze of your embroidering,
when your eyes brim with pure tears,
a haze brimming with pure tears rises,

when you think, 'If only. . .!'
a haze thinking, 'If only. . .!'
when you silently groan, 'Ah!'
a haze silently groaning, 'Ah!'

A haze rises.
Looking like sorrowful dishevelled love,
delicately trembling, it rises.

Fresh green

What ever shall I do?
Ah, I've fallen in love.
In secret, all alone, I've fallen in love!

Everywhere petals are falling;
new verdure is sprouting again
around me on every side.

Writhing in utter grief,
red petals drop and fall;
fluttering fluttering dropping, they fall

like the breath of an ancient Silla girl,
like the hair of an ancient Silla girl,
in the wind in the meadows they drop and fall.

Again this year they scatter before me,
trembling brrr they scatter. . .

Ah, I've fallen in love.
All alone I've fallen in unbearable love,
a love I can't sing in an oriole's call.

Complaint from a swing

– Chun-hyang's first monologue

Push hard on the swing, Hyang-dan,
as if launching a boat
out toward distant seas,
Hyang-dan!

as if pushing me off for ever,
away from these gently rocking willow trees,
these wild flowers like those embroidered on my pillow,
away from these tiny butterflies, these orioles,
Hyang-dan!

Push me up towards the sky:
no coral, no islands there!
Push me up like a tinted cloud!
Push up this stirring heart!

Strive as I may, I cannot go
like the moon going westward.

Push me higher and higher still,
like waves pushed up by the wind,
Hyang-dan.

Another bright day

– Chun-hyang's second monologue

Divine Spirit. . .

At first my heart
was like the haze on days when
myriads of skylarks sing.

It was like clusters of tiny drifting clouds,
or the green ripples of a river
alive with fish bright in shimmering scales.

Divine Spirit. . .

But then, one day you came to me in his form and likeness
and I was transformed into a raging whirlwind,
a waterfall hurtling over a cliff,
torrents of rain pouring down.

But then, Divine Spirit. . .

You took him away again
like the ocean swallowing tiny streams,
and in my bright empty heart
you placed the last glimmers of an evening glow.
With another long night ahead.

Divine Spirit. . .

Now
day is bright above me again,
and my heart's hue is your love,
like bellflowers in bloom up mountain valleys.

Chun-hyang's last message

– Chun-hyang's third monologue

Farewell now,
dear lord.

Fare always well, well as that leafy verdant tree
beneath whose shade we stood united
on the day of our first encounter,
the fifth day of the fifth month last.

I am not sure I know where the afterworld lies
but I cannot think it lies farther away
than Chun-hyang's love can reach.

I may flow as black water a thousand fathoms
            underground,
or waft as a cloud in the fourth heavenly sphere,
isn't that still close to my dearest lord?

When the cloud turns to rain and comes pouring down,
only think: Chun-hyang is sure to be there!

My poetry

It must have been in the spring one year, I wonder when? A long, long time ago.

I was out walking with a relative's wife when we came to a place inside the walls where a camellia tree cast its shade.

While she sat looking as if she knew exactly which portion of the sky had brought those magnificent flowers into bloom, regretfully I gathered up the fallen petals that lay strewn over the grass and laid them on the wide spreading folds of her skirt.

I repeated the action over and over again.

Many years have passed since then, and I have written poems, but always with a heart not so very different from the day I gathered up and offered those flowers.

But now, strange to say, I find there's no one in the world for me to offer them to.

So the petals I have gathered up slip softly from my grasp and tumble to the ground, but it is only with such a heart that I can write my poetry.

Beside the melting River Han

That the river should thaw!
I wonder why it's thawing again?
What griefs of ours, what joys
inspire the river to thaw again?

Like a wild goose,
like a wild goose in frosty midwinter
I longed to be gone, bewailing my life,
smashing my heart at heaven's heavy mantle of ice.

Why is the river thawing again,
giving me this sunshine and ripples?

Is it telling me to bow my head, to see again
the dandelions, the mugwort and such?

Or is it telling me to stop, to watch again
the flowered bier passing
beyond the yellow hills,
and the gathered throngs of widows?

That the river should thaw!
I wonder why it's thawing again?
What griefs of ours, what joys
inspire the river to thaw again?

In falling snow

It's -- all -- right. . .
It's -- all -- right. . .
It's -- all -- right. . .
It's -- all -- right. . .

In the heavily falling snow
a sound of tiny pheasants and quails comes nestling. . .
It's alright. . . alright. . . alright. . .
In the softly falling snow
a sound of rosy-faced maidens comes nestling. . .

A sound of
weeping
laughing
bowing
freezing blue,
of all the Fates as they're embraced.

The big ones dropping big tears,
          the small ones gurgling little laughs,
busy loving murmurs of big and small as they're embraced.

It's alright. . .
It's alright. . .
It's alright. . .
It's alright. . .

In the endlessly falling snow, the sound of the hills,
the hills, the green hills too being embraced. . .

Kwanghwa-mun

As I walked on, I saw Bugak Hill and Samgak Hill
        standing there like brother and sister;
as I walked on, I saw them standing
        like a sister behind her brother's shoulder,
then I suddenly found myself at Kwanghwa-mun.

Kwanghwa-mun, Gateway of Light,
        is indeed a lofty religion!
In times past our people always exalted the light
that drenched them: the head, the whole body, at last
        their very slippers' curving tops;
but Kwanghwa-mun is rare indeed,
solemnly bearing on its pinions an azure splendour
        overflowing from heaven above.

Above the double roof of the gate's two tiers
the sky is brimming:
what touches the upper roof runs, flows, overflows,
while an attic like a bridal room lies between the two,
so what reaches the lower roof can all come and go there.

Ready for one as lovely as jade
to live in that attic
gathering the sky.

As I slip past the walls with lowered head,
the songs heard in the streets sound so ancient, it seems,

if I suddenly look up, there, above my head,
my heart's echo, trembling and fluttering. . . .

Now spring is nearly here

That pine tree is young as you are young
and in twenty days, the plum trees will bloom.
In humus formed of thousand-year boughs
fresh orchids are rising, smooth and straight.

The second month

Under the new spring sky bamboo groves are shimmering.
As they murmur murmur murmur in the sunlight,
uttering whispered songs in the sunlight,
pretty sweet young girls grow up.

So splendid, this blossoming

So splendid, this blossoming in sunlight as spring comes.
So splendid, this pink and white blossoming of trees.
As I go down to the water, my eyes full of blossom,
petals heap up in my breast.
So splendid, this blossoming in sunlight as spring comes.

Untitled

The happiest thing of all today is the springtime sunlight shining on the greening of ancient boughs, and the fineness of fresh blades of grass beneath our walking feet. Children are being taught to utter halting words; they have a way of gazing at us with eyes like those of the children in sacred pictures. They stare at us so casually.

Prayer I

At this moment I am like an empty jar, or like an empty plain. Heaven, I beg you, put in me a terrible storm for a while, or a few fluttering butterflies, or turn me into a pot half-full of water, whatever pleases you. Now I am like a jar that was full of flowers and scents, but has just been emptied out.

Prayer II

I dreamed last night that I was sitting on a rock beside a pool at the foot of some mountain cliff, and an unknown boy was there with me. Over the pool hung a single persimmon tree, its tart half-ripe fruit dangling above the water.

Heaven! I pray you make my dreams and my waking always be like that!

Sangni Orchard

If I judge solely by its scent, the flowering orchard is a flood as sinewy as the flow of the River Han, or the upper reaches of the Naktong River. But if I glimpse the flowers' many faces one by one, I find a gale of rapturous laughter, like that of my nieces or my nieces' little friends.

Where else in the whole wide world can you find bodies like these, so gloriously exploding with inborn joy? Every single part of the pear trees, brought here from the West, is adorned with dainty clusters of flowers, not only the head and heart, but the belly and back, and right on down to the heels as well. Every morning and evening, finches, sparrows, shrikes, and orioles, with all their chicks, make themselves the mouthpieces of this huge joy; all day long, hundreds of thousands of honey bees drone their sound like the beating of big and little drums, performing a rite of thankfulness, while now and then some of their untiring throng burrow down and fall asleep amidst it all; it's all so natural!

I wonder what we ought to do, if we are intent on loving all this? Should we lie spread out beneath the trees like the water of ponds, reflecting their beauty, and from time to time receive on our bodies the childlike lightly falling petals? Or should we place ourselves apart from them, in line with the far-off hills, and watch their morning toilet, their daytime dances, and the way they sink down, melting, settling in the twilight?

Confronted by the lack of grief here, where there is nothing grieving, at least we should not teach our children to grieve. Can we find the kind of grief we far too often inflict on others in any shrike, or bird, or bee, or butterfly, as they bless the flowers, in any bud or cluster of flowers? Once all have regained their nests in early evening, and night has covered far and wide our children and ourselves, the hills and the streams, we must point out to our children the nearest stars, and let them hear the sound of the most ancient bell.

71

From a diary: at the foot of a mountain

One morning

I suddenly looked with fresh eyes at our ancient mountains. They were just squatting there, rough and stupid, oblivious, and the clouds in the sky were all the time clustering and snuggling round them; but there was no way I could understand why those clouds were pressing so closely against such repulsive old things.

Then, as I gazed at the familiar sight of them wooing each other, the next day, and the next day, and the next, I finally realized what it was all about.

It's just like when our young human couples kiss each other's cheeks, and caress one another's hair; only these gestures have been going on for perhaps several hundred thousand years! As if all that remains of earth's sordid battles has been cleansed and gone soaring up, to flow for ever over a unified jade-coloured space: perhaps the mountains have been perfomrring those constant gestures of unrestrained longing ever since they were young.

That night I heard the sound of a mountain singing in a clear ringing voice. Yes, in a darkness still as if submerged a thousand fathoms beneath the sea, I clearly heard that mountain sing.

It must have been nearly midnight. It sounded like a song sung softly by a new bride alone, venturing to open her lips only a few weeks after arriving at her husband's family home. It was the kind of song that gives a glimpse of flower-gardens seen when still a maid, and it brought their fragrance floating by. The mountain sang in a soft deep voice, seeming eager to arouse not just those flowers but even their very roots.

Can anything remain so long unforgotten? Sometimes we hear of a young widow who has stayed intact and chaste, living alone for thirty years or more in the bright clothes she wore when first she entered her dead husband's home. But for how many years has each mountain stayed in one place?

A voice as clear as that of waters that grow no older though they endure the fall of countless dynasties: such a voice can still be heard ringing in each and every mountain.

The next day,

there was a green shade which long attracted my gaze in the bright daylight, it seemed to conceal some secret. Here and there in the checkered shadows, things were whispering, glimmering pale; suddenly they were parted by what seemed to be the passing of a vast fragrance and there came thrust towards me a gilded swing bearing an elegant youth. It seemed it was intended to elevate, if not the mountain itself, at least its sons and daughters...

The Essence of Silla
1960

Queen Sondok speaks

My tomb will be in the second heaven
        of this world of desire, above verdant peaks.
There is blood here, blood here, so inevitably
clouds thicken, rain sets in, in such a heaven.

There is blood here, blood here, so never be niggardly:
the rich must carry fuel and food to the sick,
they must sometimes comfort widows and widowers,
while sturdy men must always stand on Chomsong-dae,
        on Chomsong-dae.

Lay this pure gold bracelet, the brightest
among the things that touch the flesh, on the breast
of the man driven mad by the flesh, by the flesh;
if still the troubled flames do not expire,
sing a governing song across the sea to heaven's end.

But if it is love, if it truly is love,
let it burn on for ever and ever,
longer than our laws nurtured by ancient wisdom,
longer than the flames of all our laws.

My tomb will be in the second heaven
        of this world of desire, above verdant peaks.
There is blood here, blood here, so inevitably
clouds thicken, rain sets in, in such a heaven.

I cannot leave this spot.

Flower-garden monologue

A short poem spoken by Saso

Songs are fine, but even the finest
will only rise to the clouds, then return;
your speeding horse with its flashing hooves
was brought to a halt at the edge of the sea.
Now I have lost all taste for wild boar, arrow-struck,
or those mountain birds that the falcons take.
Dear flowers, opening each dawn,
I love you dearly, dearest of all;
yet, like a child unable to swim
viewing its face in the water's gaze,
I simply stand leaning against the door you have closed.
Open the door. Open the door, dear flowers.
Though the way ahead lies through fire and flood,
Open the door. Open the door, dear flowers.

Saso's second letter: a fragment

One autumn day in the year after Saso first left
for the mountains, her hawk came flying with a
second letter for her father bound to its leg. This was
written, not with a bird's blood, but with a finger
dipped in the juice of fragrant plants. The paper was
once again from the roll of mulberry paper she had
taken from home.
This is all that remains of the first half of
the letter:

I have recovered now from the disease
       that caused the buzzing in my blood.

This spring
my hawk
spied out a misty field, a little patch
emerald green like a river of perfume;

that was five or six months ago, today
my blood rustled like pink clover bushes
then burst into flames like jade-green starlight,
unfolding to the skies a vein of living gold.

Father,
it unfolds that vein of living gold to the skies for you,
for my little Bulgonae, for Bulgonae's unknown father,
and for all the young girls who will come after us
in a thousand far off, distant years.

Silla merchandise

Here's something a falcon can always find with its keen eyes.

Suppose it's light like a scrap of cotton, if it's placed in the corner of a courtyard where a falcon can spot it, the bird will always be able to pick it up from the house of whoever buys it.

The falcon, our companion, knows about such things from before, from when they lived at home. It knows from seeing them as it goes soaring up and down: Pine Mountain to the East, Diamond Mountain to the North, Wuji to the South, Pijon to the West.

Open your eyes and look! This cotton was your daughter's own flower, out in the cotton field.

Open your eyes, and look! This rice was gathered, was gathered at your son's own seedbed.

Tori! Tori! Tori! Tori! Rotting away to dust, now!

That was the song we used to sing!

The bridge

In the eighth month of the twelfth year of King Silsong,
clouds were seen shrouding the hills;
they seemed to be inhabited lofts,
perfumes surging through every room.

One day, one was borne on a bier along mountain paths
but, not forgetting, he returned again
to the village, searched in strangers' hearts;
then, it being a beautiful day,
a beautiful day,
he went to dwell in a summer lodge earlier prepared.

Leading some souls of the tinier kind that crawl on
        the earth
he took a path of mist above the clear hills
and went to dwell in that summer lodge;

he had promised that lodge with his living breath,
        the clear breath of his living days;
it was completed in beauty in the spurting flames
        of his funeral pyre,
and he went to dwell
in that lodge
that lodge
that lodge.

The people of Silla celebrated the event,
making the forest beneath the cloud grow thick;
and, to make it easier to reach that lodge,
below it they built a bridge of stones.

Hundred-patch: a song

Old Hundred-patch, of Saemal near Nangsan,
was so poor that his clothes were patched again and again,
they looked like quails tied together with string;
hence people made that name for him.

But that man had a cunning lyre
that he had long possessed and played,
and with it he cheered his heart so much
that even Poverty could never outpace him
but plodded obediently on behind.
Day after day he rose like the sun
and lived untroubled as a stream.

One year, late on New Year's Eve, his wife
could hear the crunch of millet being pounded fine
in the house next door, and before she knew it
a word slipped past: 'Hulled millet!'
Then the lyre rang out, expunged the word,
and ebbed away again like water.

The sun

In the glorious days of great Silla,
when Adalla was king,
the sun came to the loom of Yono's wife, Seyo,
and stayed dangling there, for she had begun
     by fixing her warp-ties to the sky.
Anywhere she and the silk went, the sun would follow
     after.
The people of Silla all knew this, so when one day
they found she had been carried off to Japan on a rock,
they pursued her and brought back a ship
     loaded with that cloth of silk.

The old man who offered flowers

I'll leave the cow I'm leading
here beside the crimson rock
and I'll pick those flowers for you,
if you're not embarassed by me.

These words were once addressed
by an old man of Silla to a certain young woman.

I'll leave the cow I'm leading
here beside the crimson rock
and I'll pick those flowers for you,
if you're not embarassed by me.

A warm sunny day, springtime of course,
beneath the cliff lovely with azaleas stands
that grey-haired old man leading his cow when
suddenly he sees someone's wife passing before him
and addresses these words to her.

Had he quite forgotten his own white beard
and how old he was?

Of course.
All forgotten.

Had he quite forgotten she was someone's wife
and everything else?

Of course.
All forgotten.

He had nothing left at all except a feeling
like that of a flower laughing for joy
at the sight of another flower.

*

Between the mounted husband and their escort
the wife was likewise riding on horseback.

Oh, look, how lovely, those flowers!
If only someone would bring me some!

She seemed to speak to the flowers,
to the people, and the air as well.

The husband heard the words uttered by his wife
as she swayed along on her horse's back
but foolishly dismissed them,
the servants too just let them glide past,
while an old man from another clan
overheard what she said as he passed, responded
and uttered these words.

I'll leave the cow I'm leading
here beside the crimson cliff
and I'll pick those flowers for you,
if you're not embarassed by me.

The flowers grew at the summit of a cliff:
had he forgotten how high it was, even?
Of course.
How high or low
all forgotten.
All he could see and feel was
how utterly familiar
the air was becoming, in today's terms,
drenching their lips and ears and eyes
drenching their words and speech,
that utterly
limpid
air.

Ancient poem I

If somewhere a strong rope is hanging from the sky,
if deep in some well a long road stretches far away,
if I can become the east wind, or any wind at all,
I will go, anyway, though I have to clamber or swim.
I will go, anyway, through a gap in the door,
  a crack in the wall.
But if you have turned to bitter ashes before my eyes,
  how shall I return?
If you have turned to a watery flood,
  how shall I return?

Ancient poem II

Where a chrysanthemum blooms then vanishes,
a chrysanthemum spirit arises and lives;

where a clover-bush blooms then vanishes,
a clover spirit arises and lives;

where a deer plays then vanishes,
a deer spirit arises and lives;

if you visit grandmother's village beyond the hills,
where the flowers she saw have vanished,
a host of the spirits of the flowers she saw. . .

where flower spirits live then vanish,
more flower spirits' spirits emerge and live;

where deer spirits live then vanish,
those spirits' spirits emerge and live.

In Chinju

Have you ever seen a cloud the colour and size
of a crape-myrtle flower hanging in the sky?

I did once, in Chinju, during the Retreat of January '50.

Have you ever seen a couple of zelkova trees
that have lived together for five hundred years
        with never a row?

I did once, in Chinju, during the Retreat of January '50.

Have you ever seen a *kisaeng* become a pure river's spirit,
one really alive?

I did once, in Chinju, during the Retreat of January '50.

A new bride was dipping her hands in Non-gae's river:
'If you rub your skin with it, every disease is cured.'
The poet Sol Chang-su pointed, and I saw.

Sook Yong-i becomes a butterfly

*According to an old tale, as Sook Yong-i arrived
before the tomb of her fiancé, Yang San-i, the tomb
split apart and gaped open. A relative standing there
tried to prevent her from rushing headlong in, by
seizing the fringe of her skirt, but it tore off and
remained for a moment dangling, then turned into
a butterfly.*

That butterfly is still alive.
That butterfly is still alive, that appeared
after Sook Yong-i and Yang San-i had fixed the day
to unite their lives only Yang San-i left this world before,
so Sook Yong-i went rushing after him.
Above the tomb that gaped at the power of her love,
hovering beside the person who seized her clothes,
that butterfly, that emerged from the torn-off fringe
of Sook Yong-i's skirt, is still alive today.

Waiting

My waiting is over.
The last person I had been expecting
has passed beyond this jujube tree bend;
now there is no one left for me to wait for.

I take early summer, now past, and bright autumn days,
this jujube tree, too,
that was only dream leaves, fruit of life's reward,
and thrust them all into the life to come.
My waiting is over.

A whisper

Madame, your muted whispers
are as quiet as persimmon trees in July
and yet, Madame, I think
there's really no need for you to whisper so.
Even the prettiest of all your brood
will never be more than the fret it is now:
how could it ever learn to whisper?

Cute rhymes

Sister, elder sister dear,
dark and smart as sesame cake,
all I've got is new as new,
nothing of mine is faded yet;
so sister, elder sister dear,
sister dark as deepest night,
let me hug you once again,
shadows round your eyes and all.

A pomegranate opens

Lady, when you were in your prime,
in youthful ardour I ventured a marriage proposal;
you knew then, and you know now, too,
I'm just a poor though honest scholar. . .
Autumn's come, why are you opening the gate?
You would send me to escort one of your many daughters,
a mature one, on a distant wedding journey?
I have only the stepping-stones in the village there,
what shall I ride on to follow her?

Juniper tree

Tree, tree, sweet juniper tree!
Oh sweet tree, sweet juniper tree!
Before the gate where my love is coming,
sweet tree, sweet juniper tree!

If you ask me to live by a lowly hedge, a window frame,
wearing a veil too thin to warm a one-eyed man,
if you ask me to live indoors with the windows closed,
if you ask me to live indoors, lamps lit, just the two of us,

not a soul in men's or women's quarters, no one to be
        aware,
in your vivid songs of love ten thousand years will pass;
not a soul in men's or women's quarters, no one to be
        aware,
in your vivid songs of love ten thousand years will pass.

Tree, tree, sweet juniper tree!
Oh sweet tree, sweet juniper tree!
Before the gate where my love is coming,
sweet tree, sweet juniper tree!

Uncle Jinyong: a portrait

Uncle Jinyong in our village is so handy with a plough,
like a pretty maid eating a pear,
like a pretty maid eating a pear,
he seems to be ploughing mist, on his way to get wed.

Beneath his morning-star top-knot pin, he has sidewhiskers
like a grove of bush-clover shrubs, of bush-clover shrubs,
bushy as the clover-brush his missus holds
as she sweeps their courtyard, front and back.

Like a field-side shelter over blustery breezes
once the flowers have bloomed and melon-time comes;
like river-waters where grey mullet leap
when their growth is done and mullet-time comes;

under the village tree a checker-board's set out,
old and young are all shouting advice;
reaching over their shoulders, he puts pieces askew:
it looks just like a coffin-board.

To Autumn

Come!
You who are still capable of love.
Now is the time for pale and fragile doors to open
in each corner of the garden you're banished from.

Come!
You who smoulderingly resist vulgarity. Now's the moment
when you must set out ahead of the skeins of wild geese,
departing with your wrinkles of desolate care intact.
Grieving glorious, solitary brother, now is the time to
        begin;
brother autumn, you must set out now with brow and
        breast.

In the place where last year our last flower bloomed,
that final chrysanthemum, this year a new one strives to
        rise,
eager to ease as September chills drive us into October
        frost.

Come!
Clouds set in order.
Clouds set in order after erring and idling,
you can't retain us now with the poppy's bloodstained
        tales;
bright unfolding must begin again from the gate at the
        back,
and each morning raise up frost-buried faces
to harden us.

Come!
You who are still capable of love.
Now is the time for pale and fragile doors to open
in each corner of the garden you're banished from.

When I was five

I first had a taste of solitude when I was five.

For some reason my parents went away for a whole day, leaving me alone at home; for a time I sat on the wooden floor, banging my feet up and down, then I laid my head on the fulling block and slept. It was when I awoke, that something first began to draw me: it seemed I was being swept towards an ocean into which I was unwilling to be plunged. In the ocean, was that a cuckoo? I had heard the name from my mother but knew nothing of its shape: in, in, in, and its calling increased like the scores of verdant lanterns gleaming in the lotus-lamp night of Buddha's Birth, fanning the feeling in my sinking surroundings and the floor beneath.

I jumped down and went to stand by the little brook that flowed outside the brushwood gate. The nightmare I had just been plunged in, still making a thin keening noise, grew calm as it was mirrored in the smooth water beneath the smartweed; then it joined the cotton clouds floating above and began quietly to draw close against my sides and breast, like the paper jacket my mother used to make and wear on the night before each year's first full moon.

Untitled

Mary, now my love can only become
a hue to colour your bright halo.
Until that day when you first loomed before me,
a stream piercing the darkness, there'd been nothing
but a poor rabble of acrobats prancing about my stage
like a patch of barley-blossom fresh on Buddha's Nativity;
blood is more, so it was all a sickening, unbearable waste.
Mary.
This blood seems about to dance and give off sparks:
it could be distilled into a liquor like the wine we offer
on summer days; or, if even that is found unworthy,
might be made into feed, following you, friend, at last. . .
can only become blue and white hues
to colour your bright halo.

Forty

Beside the pond there were two seats,
I sat down close beside you
but I love you was not once spoken; it remained
like the echoes of a scale rising in a mute's mind,
so that nothing more was possible,
I only ventured gradually up the scale, note by note;
I wonder how far you followed me?
A few moments later, you were no longer there.

After that I preferred walking,
first on a path that wound away from that pond,
then on a path that wound away from that path,
then on a path that went yet further away from that.

But nowadays, setting out on my morning stroll,
as I walk along, I must admit the thought quite often comes
of going once more by way of the pond.

Untitled

I'll become a bell, perhaps; I will if I have to.
Hung high up as I used to ring

here at this crossroads
this four-branched crossroads
with the sun setting
as twilight deepens

I'll become a bell, perhaps; I will if I have to.
ringing out with a cracked sound if I crack

I don't know how you feel,
I'm anxious, that's all,
so anxious
that I'm melting, that's all.

Though I ring a thousand years at your house's threshold,
I'll become a bell perhaps; I will if I have to.

Even if I make a foul sound now
having cracked and fallen
after lingering and calling
round the castle walls in younger days;

I'll become a bell, perhaps; I will if I have to.
I'll become a bell, perhaps; I will if I have to.

Untitled

Anyway, it's certain there's something I've lost.
Taking a gourd dipper,
one fit for the weakling I am,
suppose I try scooping up sea water here?

There's no bolt-hole up in the stars;
if I galloped off on some Australian horse,
there'd be no fraying of veils, I know!
Water gathers, rustling and stale
like my faded blood
and maybe now I'm only pretending
to scoop up this sea water.

Is it like what arises when flesh touches flesh?
If your hand is short, then mine should be long,
if my hand is short, then yours should be long,
or was there no contact, despite the efforts we made?
Anyway, it's certain there's something I've lost.

Untitled

Like rubbing cheek against cheek, that's what it's like!
The teasiness shown by the west wind, southern breezes,
bleak gusts, all the winds, unable to leave,
is like rubbing cheek against cheek, that's what it's like!

Hills, blue hills, less worn than I, who've been wearing out
since the days of the Three Wise Emperors long ago;
hills less worn, younger than I am, and taller too:

when my life is done and at last I join you,
the winds will embrace us, toss us, toss
until we turn to pebbles of quartz.
Hills, one day you'll turn to pebbles of quartz
patterning almost invisible me.

Those pebbles, too, after sitting about like coquetry,
will turn into finest finest grains of sand.
And the dust of those grains will become red clay.

Then, hills, then
we'll lie together,
the oldest of all old things,
and sustain the waving grass in the fields.

Like rubbing cheek against cheek, that's what it's like!
The teasiness shown by the west wind, southern breezes,
bleak gusts, all the winds, unable to leave,
is like rubbing cheek against cheek, that's what it's like!

One afternoon

Half past three,
no one here to laugh:
in the western sky,
a single cloud
flat on its belly!
Just like you in the old days,
sprawled on the warmest spot in the room,
a cloud flat on its belly, flat on its belly!
Why, it can't come or go or stand up either!
That cloud sprawled flat on its belly!

November riddle

Do you know the path I follow with pale fretted brow,
the path the wild geese take in late autumn migrations?
A path fit for a ha'penny mandarin, forgotten for a moment
at summer's arrowroot tangles, autumn's clover-bush
        passes:
stretching north again now November shines bright!
November, when my new wild goose path grimly opens,
the month a new goose path kindles open in my study.

One late autumn day

Like Spinoza, who in times of hardship would grind lenses for glasses,

the heavens polish the rocky walls along the way that opens before me.

One day in late autumn I came to a sudden halt among the tawny fields of cogon grass, fields worn down by countless passings, where nothing but bare tough stems remained.

First a banquet in emerald green, then fragrance, then a pair of hempen sandals for our feet that finally got tossed to the roadside, quite worn out, manifesting nothing but their tattered cords. . .

and this resolve, this resolve, looking for all the world like a worn out straw sole.

All was because of this resolve, plainly manifesting one last time its inmost cords.

Faint autumn murmurs

The persimmons by the fence are tinted tart,
the cockscomb and hollyhock are tinted scarlet:
so what tint am I, this autumn day?

Last year's gourd lies like a big fist in the garden,
the dipper's lying outside like a small fist:
so where should my fist best be laid?

After a fast

My today
has come and settled
like the sacred bowls on a mica-bright altar

and before my mountain
the host of young crape-myrtle flowers
has sent laughter flowing like water into my heart.

Sent flowing like water into my heart,
it has become one more blossoming cluster of flowers
and now goes surging on towards you.

As lanterns are kindled
on nights in May for Buddha's birth,
so it goes kindled, kindled, kindled, it goes.

My today
has come and settled in a village near you
like the sacred bowls on a mica-bright altar

and is going like a pheasant to visit your home.
It's going on its visit
sending skywards sounds going to a field of reeds.

A brief astronomical history of Korea

Between fifteen hundred and a thousand years ago,
          a star came down,
eager to help youths climbing Diamond Mountain
and it would sweep the path before their feet.
But after the teachings of the Sung masters arrived
it returned, took a position higher than a hand could reach
until civilized Japanese arrived and plastered the space
between star and hand full of emptiness.
Single-handed I drew near to it
and by means of a vein inside my body
I drew it down into my guts,
where I thought its path was cut.
This morning at dawn the star came spilling out.
After spilling out, it dropped down again
and flowed through me; after flowing through me
it came spilling out once more.
I shall have to mend my bowels again.

Between two juniper trees

Like the sun dangling between two junipers,
chi ching chi dah ching
dear heart,
now make a sound of gold or silver.

My bride is no longer water or blood, now,
but a hovering mist looming darkly blue,
drawn up from a final bed of flowers!

Though I go on and on, every path only inclines
to what you may call the Golden Land of the West,
or what name you will, there's no other way.

Dear heart! Dear heart!
Take your seared bride as seared as yourself,
a gaunt and skinny vein, this morning:
chi ching chi dah ching
make a sound of gold or silver.

A letter

Sunshil! My boyhood friend,
do you remember
those childhood days, like torrents surging
newly emerging tumbling down some mountain gorge,
with a yearning for the soaring swing fastened there?

And Sunshil,
I hope you still preserve our love
still brimming, if only feebly, from those days?

Later,
like a flimsy-winged butterfly wandering
sometimes I settled on living trees
but mostly perched on dead trees and marshes.

Sunshil!
You must be full of wrinkles by now! Tonight,
sitting on a sandy shore twinkling dragonfly-bright eyes
are you spreading sublime emerald-green starlight?

I've alighted on almost every tree, alive and dead,
perched on almost every wild field and pit;
now, uniting times of wrinkled love,
          as numerous as your wrinkles and mine,
let's meet again as in childhood days
when the daylight Milky Way shone in every budding
          lotus.
Let's meet again as in childhood days.

A lonely journey

When I stopped beneath the first casement
it was a bed of blood-red peonies;

but when I arrived at the second casement
it had become, not blood, not blood,
from the surging falling streams
it had become the sea.

Tell me, stars, you stars and sun, you moon and stars,
when the oceans wear out and mount to the sky,
when they wear out like quartz and mount to the sky,
do they turn into sun and moon? Do they turn into stars?

On the third window was lingering a sound,
a sound of seas wearing out that mount to the sky,
seas wearing out like quartz, a sound trembling with dread.
On the third window was lingering
a cloud of steam streaming from a boiling cauldron,
white steam and azure, a cloud of love.

But reluctant to go, rigged out in this flesh,
I travel on and on, the journey's unending,
endless this journey, driven on overwhelmed,

and now my lonely thoughts become a breeze
ready to serve my onflowing brothers as a guide,
bringing tidings in due season to flowering boughs,
tidings to past sweethearts' casement-sides,
closing around the months and days, then returning.
Becoming a breeze without eyes, nose or breath,
they come back again as my brothers' guide.

The sea

Giddy they seem, ever bounding, curling, those billows
tartly tart,
unbound locks dishevelled flying, no other skill.

If we go a little deeper, solids are solid. Punishments
punish.
Conclusions at last are conclusions, ends end.

Finally haphazardly trampling the meadows, in ranks
like hemp fields
like hemp fields,
with no place to go, wherever they go,
confinement's eternal interlinked cubes
under heaven's retribution!
All hail, the sea!
All hail, the sea!
All hail, the sea, the sea, the sea!

To what end did you come hurtling down?
To what end did you perch there, watery dancing child?
To what end did you come cascading down?
Exposed like meat on a butcher's slab,
why did you come hurtling over the brink? Come hurtling?
Perhaps to deck bridal rooms?
Not with blood
but with water, with ever so silently silent water,
the blood's totality's ultimate reason's purification,
perhaps now to deck the bridal rooms in place?

Until you become a billowing cloud, a billowing cloud
by the steam of love rising from a cauldron
where a fowl's being boiled.
Ah sea!

In suburban mud

The colour of this muddy pool is like the colour
of your brows, on days you're sick and haven't washed,
        but
this is a paste of rotting bones, flesh flour, and faded
        blood.
Expert! Expert!
Your muscles have been training for this a whole life long.
Like errands, thefts, or beggars, even!
Your wits have been busy training for this a whole life
        long.
Like being a house-maid, or a whore, a whore!
If ever I get involved in this,
it has a skill of sticking there and getting stuck.

Above all, what about sowing seeds, raising pigs,
or fattening girls to marry off?
Or feeding a kid as a foster son?
Right. The plan is to rig him in scholar's garb,
and see him graduate from Seoul National University,
making a purist of him;
so no shirking, now!

112

Ballad of the cuckoo

From the very first day my love for you
was never a heavenly love, I confess.
I stole you for the Heaven I glimpsed
simply, so simply contained within you,
simply held upon your flesh;
oh, everyone knows about my theft.
Wife, my wife, my runaway wife,
your present heavenly dwelling
is better than any cuckoo, I know.
Our new-born baby takes more after you
than after me, yes, that's for sure.
So as I sob here, whimpering for grief,
if I crumble whimpering, if I turn to dust
and somehow that dust gets wafted aloft
and clings to your side, for lost love's sake
do not brush it away, but let it be;
for that's how things were in former days
near the upper and lower Eight Mountain Pools.

Song of Karma-destiny

Once I bloomed as a peony flower.
Nearby, in sight of me, there lived a pretty maid.

At last, once day
my petals dropped to the ground; they lay there,
they dried; and so with time they turned to dust,
were united with the clay.
Just then, the little girl died too,
they buried her in the ground nearby.
Soon the rain came pouring down,
swept away the dust, the ashes of the peony flower;
that water poured into a flowing stream,
and the blood of the maid who now lay in the ground
trickled too into that selfsame stream.

The peony dust floating in the stream
entered the guts of a passing fish
and soon became part of the fish's flesh;
just then the maid's lost blood that had trickled down
was caught in a wave that rippled close by the fish.
The fish leaped for joy, at which the poor thing
was caught and eaten by a water-bird flying just above;
a moment more, and the blood of the maid was drawn up
by the sunbeams' might, went rising into the sky and
                    became
a cloud caressing that bird's feathered wings.

One day a hunter's arrow struck the bird
and down it went, dropping to the ground;
the cloud begged it to stay but that could not be.
The cloud conceived and fell as rain
on the garden of the people who had bought the bird.
That couple ate the bird that night, digested it,
then begot a child, that was born and grew.
Meanwhile the shower had thawed a seed,
a peony seed, buried in the ground;
it sprouted, it grew, and began to flower.

At last in the garden the day has come
for the newly sprung plant to blossom its best.
Look! Flower and maid in sight of each other again!
only today the maid is alive in the flower, while
the former peony is now looking out, a part of me.

Notes

Self-portrait (page 2)

The Year of Reforms: 1894 saw a radical reform of the Korean systems of law and government; this year is named 'Gap-O' in the traditional cycle of names for each year. The same year saw the start of the Dong-hak Uprising, so it might also be translated as 'the Year of Revolt.'

A leper (page 4)

There was a superstitious belief that a leper could be healed by eating human flesh.

A postcard sent to Dong Ri (page 15)

Dong Ri is the novelist Kim Dong Ri.

Ko Eul-na's daughter (page 19)

Just outside the southern gate of the city of Cheju, on the island of the same name, visitors are shown a cavern out of which the three spirits Ko Eul-na, Bu Eul-na, and Yang Eul-na, are said to have emerged. These were venerated as the founding ancestors of the three families bearing their names, and as the founders of the island's Tamra Kingdom.

My Rooster I (page 20)

Chigui Isle is a small island not far from Soguipo in Cheju, the island province to the south of Korea.

Resurrection (page 25)

Chongno is the name of one of Seoul's main streets.

The Herdsman's song (page 32)

The Herdsman and the Lady Weaver are the two stars Altair and Vega, at opposite ends of the Milky Way. There is an Oriental legend telling how, after they married, they were punished for spending time together when they should have been working. They were allowed to meet only once a year, on the 7th day of the 7th lunar month, walking across the Milky Way on a bridge known as O-jak-kyo (Crows and Magpies Bridge). The rain that often falls on that day is thought to come from their tears.

A song of the Goddess of Mercy in the Stone Cavern (page 34)

In a hill not far from Kyongju, in south-eastern Korea, there is a granite statue of Buddha in an artificial cavern called Sokuram. Other ancient carvings surround the central seated Buddha. The Goddess (or Boddhisatva) of Mercy is called Kwanum or Kwanseum in Korean, Avalokitesvara in Sanskrit.

Nightingale (page 36)

This bird, which figures very often in Chinese and Korean poetry under a variety of names, is not the same bird as the European nightingale. Its Latin name is Otus scops stictonotus and in appearance it is a typical owl. Its plaintive call is associated with sunset and nightfall. Its name 'Kwi-chok-do' (way back to Shu) comes from a tale of the emperor of the Chinese empire of Shu, who died in captivity in a neighbouring land. His homesick soul became this bird. The bird's tongue is blood-red and this has inspired beliefs that it drinks its own blood, and that it sings itself to death. It is often confused in

Korean folklore with the cuckoo, and some translators use that word.

Returning to Soguipo (page 42)

Soguipo is a town on Cheju, an island province lying south of the Korean Peninsula.

Why do I so want to live? (page 52)

The lines at the head of the poem are by O Il-do (1901-1946), one of the founders of modern Korean lyric poetry.

The lines of verse inserted in the text (pages 50-1) are taken from two folk-songs. The first is a lament at the arrival of the corpse of a husband or sweetheart who has died away from home. The second evokes the life-giving flowers that are thought to grow in the Western Paradise, the Elysian Fields of Oriental legend.

On seeing Mudung Mountain (page 56)

Mudung Mountain is on the outskirts of the south-western city of Kwangju.

Haze (page 59)

Kongdok-dong and Malli-dong are the names of two neighbourhoods in Seoul.

Complaint from a swing, etc. (pages 61, 62, 63)

Chun-hyang is the heroine of a popular Korean tale of love. She remains faithful while her lover, Mong-ryong, is away for years of study, despite terrible attacks on her virtue by a local magistrate. In the end Mong-

118

ryong returns and they are reunited. Hyang-dan is Chun-hyang's maid and companion. The lovers first meet when Chun-hyang is on a swing.

Kwanghwa-mun (page 67)

Kwanghwa-mun is the name of the gateway in the centre of Seoul that originally opened onto the court-yard and throne-room of the main royal palace of Kyongbok-kung. Demolished by the Japanese, the gate and its complex upper pavillions have been rebuilt but the Japanese-era Capitol Building (now the National Museum) still rises obtrusively behind it. Bugak and Samgak hills rise to the north of Seoul.

Queen Sondok speaks (page 76)

Queen Sondok of Silla, knowing that a man named Chigui had fallen in love with her, came to him as he lay sleeping and laid her bracelet on his breast to comfort him. (Poet's note)

The Chomsong-dae observatory in the old Silla capital of Kyongju is said to have been built in Queen Sondok's reign.

Flower-garden monologue (page 77)

Saso (more often called Paso) was the mother of the first Silla king, Park Hyok-kose. While still a virgin she became pregnant, and withdrew into a mountain where she became a hermit; this poem represents a monologue spoken in her garden before she left her home.

Saso's second letter (page 78)

See *Samguk Yusa* 114. Bulgonae is the name of Saso's mysterious child better known as Park Hyok-kose, the mythical progenitor of the Silla royal family.

The sun (page 82)

Carried off to Japan on a rock: see *Samguk Yusa: Legends and History of the Three Kingdoms of Ancient Korea.* 22.

The old man who offered flowers (page 83)

This incident is described in *Samguk Yusa* 40, which gives the words spoken by the woman and by the old man. The woman is the Lady Suro.

In Chinju (page 87)

The Retreat of January 1950 was the lowest point in the Korean War, when the North Korean army advanced almost to the foot of the Peninsula. Chinju is near the southern coast, not far from Pusan.

Non-gae is a Korean heroine of the late 16th century, when the Japanese invaded Korea. She was an entertainer (*kisaeng*) who, in 1593, leaped to her death from the castle walls above the Nam-kang (South River) in Chinju, dragging down with her the Japanese general Keyamura.

When I was five (page 96)

The birth or Nativity of the Buddha is celebrated in Korea on the eighth day of the fourth lunar month, as the festival of Buddha's Coming. It almost always falls within the month of May in the western calendar. It is also mentioned in *Untitled* (page 91) and *After a fast* (page 100).

Ballad of the cuckoo (page 113)

A woodcutter was able to gain a heavenly nymph as his wife by stealing her garments while she bathed, but he was warned never to let her see those clothes until she had had three children. Yielding to her pleading, he gave her a glimpse of them after only two children had been born; she seized the two children in her arms and soared heavenwards. Later the woodcutter was able to win her back.

Bibliography

The most recent edition of the complete poems of So Chong Ju was published in two volumes by Minum-sa (Seoul, Korea) in 1991.

A number of So Chong Ju's poems, most of them written later than those found in the present volume, have been translated into English by Professor David R. McCann of Cornell University:

Unforgettable Things: Poems by So Chongju (Si-sa-yong-o-sa, Seoul, 1986)

Selected Poems of So Chongju (Columbia University Press, 1989)

Poems by So Chong Ju, translated by a number of different writers, have been published from time to time in the Korea Journal, published by the Korean National Commission for UNESCO. These are listed on page 71 of the Korea Journal Index 1961-1991.

The article by Professor Taedong Lee which provided the main ideas for the Introduction was published in English in the Korea Journal in December 1978:

Lee Tae-dong, 'The Poetic Reconciliation of Present and Eternal: A Study of the Modern Korean Poet So Chong-ju,' Vol. 18: 12, pp. 45-52.

An English version exists of the Buddhist chronicle history of Korea to which reference is made in the notes:

Samguk Yusa: Legends and History of the Three Kingdoms of Ancient Korea, Written by Ilyon, Translated by Ha Tae-Hung, Grafton K. Mintz, 1972, Yonsei University Press, Seoul, Korea.

Other Korean Titles
Published by Forest Books
translated by Brother Anthony of Taizé

WASTELANDS OF FIRE
Poems by Ku Sang

Ku Sang was born into a Catholic family in Seoul, grew up in what is now North Korea, studied in Japan, and after fled to the south before the Korean war. Later, in the fifties, he was imprisoned for writing essays on the corruption of power. The poetry is like the man, humble in its simplicity, rich in philosophy.

ISBN 0-948259-82-5   paper   £7.95   144pp

A KOREAN CENTURY
A sequence of poems by Ku Sang

RIVER and FIELDS are two Oriental images of time:
The river – life's linear and unreturning flow.
the fields – nature's cyclical self-renewal. Ku Sang's concern is to reconcile the two, and express a metaphysics of Christian hope within the simplicity of Oriental nature poetry, a Zen-like lightness in a daily journey from death to Resurrection.

ISBN 1-85610-001-4   paper   £7.95   128pp

FAINT SHADOWS OF LOVE
Poems by Kwang-kyu Kim

Among modern Korean poets Kwang-kyu Kim is an exception: many explode in cries of resentment and anger at all the suffering that Korea has experienced from dictatorship, war and division, industrialisation, urbanisation, but his poems are full of delicate irony. Their satire is the more devastating for being so quietly stated. He is the first Korean poet to deal with ecological themes and he wittily dissects all alienations.

ISBN 1-85610-000-6   paper   £7.95   112pp